BELLY

(Steven Schreiner)

For Michael,
a fine young poet
with a future,
amjoy all fin
dreams

Steve
STLPC
10 April 2016

Červená Barva Press
Somerville, Massachusetts

Červená Barva Press
P.O. Box 440357
W. Somerville, MA 02144-3222

www.cervenabarvapress.com

Bookstore: www.thelostbookshelf.com

Cover art: Ethan Shaltout and Steven Schreiner

Cover Design: William J. Kelle

ISBN: 978-0-9861111-8-1

Library of Congress Control Number: 2015948694

Distributed by Small Press Distribution: www.spdbooks.org

ACKNOWLEDGMENTS

My thanks to the editors of the following publications in which these poems first appeared:

Anthem ("Heartless," "Scat"); *Delmar* ("Belly," "Sympathy"); *Colorado Review* ("Vichy"); *Crab Orchard Review* ("Desolated," "Trade"); *Gulf Coast* ("Forecast"); *Flood Stage: An Anthology of St Louis Poets* ("After the Rain"); *Image: A Journal of the Arts and Religion* ("Failed Attempt"); *Margie* ("This Little Piggy"); *Naugatuck River Review* ("The Bond"); *Red Mountain Review* ("My Wife's Black Bra"); *River Styx* ("Barren," "Honeymoon," "Outside the Bath"); *Sou'wester* ("Cheat"); *Spillway* ("Poem about a thumb"); *Stosvet: Cardinal Points* ("Silk," "Steppe," "The Snow"); *Tar River Poetry* ("The Last Nile Flood"); *The 2River View* ("At the Artists' Colony"); *UCity Review* ("Nothing Goes Here"); *Winter Harvest: Jewish Writing in St. Louis 2006-2011* ("Even in a Dream the Dead are like the Photograph Still in the Camera").

The poems "Barren" and "Heartless" were reprinted in *Winter Harvest: Jewish Writing in St. Louis 2006-2011*.

For their friendship and help, I would like to thank Eric Pankey, Jennifer Atkinson, Allison Funk and Jason Sommer; George Fortier, Joy Katz, and Jeffrey Zuckerman; my deepest gratitude to Charles Baxter, Richard Newman, and Jeff Hamilton. To Jeff Friedman I owe a great debt; Howard Schwartz has always been my champion; I am grateful to the VCCA and Tall Rock Writers Retreat for opportunities to write; and to Richard Kleiman, always. To Mona, after all, and to Ethan, forever young.

For my family.

TABLE OF CONTENTS

1.

2.

3.

4.

5.

6.

BELLY

1.

The heart hopes, and hopes lie.

—Shibab Al-Deen Al-Sahrourdy

Trade

Daddy is driving the red car
which is the color of worry,
on the Garden State Parkway
when the front tire blows.
The car fights but he wrestles it
to the side of the road.
We bump to rest
like an apple under the trees.

I am bored
but hopeful, as though we are going
somewhere more important
than Howard Johnson's for dinner
after visiting another
stranger he knows well.
But the evening begins
to feel full of misery
as though we are done
with the pretense of a family
for another day.

           He lies down
on his back across the front seat,
his feet on the ground
as if to take a nap. As usual
he wears his gray wool trousers,
black Ban Lon and silk
socks, the shoes I've shined
until they were perfect
but now I see the scuff of a cloud
in their toes. My brother and I
stand stiffly beside our mother,
dutiful and beleaguered,
before the open trunk.
A stranger stops to help us.
He raises the car with one arm
and while it tips to the side
we all stand

in the shadow of the trees.

My stepfather comes forward
to give the man a gift, a box
of what he sells
to make his living: gherkin pickles
in dusty bottles, warty green
with vinegar, the rind
of watermelon, cloudy as the sea;
sweet potatoes swimming
in amber syrup, and cocktail mixes
without the booze. For the holidays
yet to come
glassy maraschino cherries
too sweet to eat,
bloodshot
cocktail onions
and a handshake.
The tools of his trade.

This Little Piggy

He was biggest, headstrong, headed for
a ham; next stayed home, tall and lean
and maybe, as toes go, handsome
as a salesman or a doctor, like my uncles.

One was fattened on roast beef, another,
his equal if a little
bent and fated to be calloused,
had none. There was I, the one she loved

most, the one she treated to a smile
and a wriggle, wrung between her fingers
till I rang with a gleeful peal.
Whether I was good or bad

or if I went to bed at seven on a summer evening
when the ringleader of a TV circus
said it was time
for all good boys and girls to go to bed

didn't matter; though I tiptoed
to listen from the bathroom floor,
the beast below awoke.
First a low rumble

stirred the air. In the dark
I could hear the turning wheels of the house
as it tumbled toward market. Then her voice
would free itself, like laughter

but more a whinny in fear
of fire. He called to her
but she did not answer, called
and called, until he was roaring *Hoor,*

hoor, hoor, as if he couldn't find her
hiding in the corner. Then
the whole house shook

like the jungle floor.

I lay my face on the tiles, where I kissed
the flinty grit and the dark mold
and the smooth, flawless skin
of her face.

Heartless

In East Orange, just off the Parkway,
I couldn't pass the cemetery

without trying to hold my breath.
In the midst of life we are in death.

Today, I saw the widow's neck
bare as the glare on the glass. Check.

Remembered my mother, myself, my brother
driving through March snow together

first in a line behind the hearse.
I didn't think it was wrong to curse

now that you were dead, your face
enclosed in the dark, your thoughts erased

except for regret. I worried that
I'd see your Borsalino hat

in the hall closet when I was alone.
Would you know? Could you atone?

I passed the escort, the sound of a boat,
and the balaclava at his throat

solemnized his ivory Harley.
The grass of an office park waved like barley.

I remembered us gathered under a tent,
my mother in a chair, the way the casket leant

slightly lower on one end, slung
between straps and castors. Kaddish sung.

And then we turned around to greet
the faces. Goodbye. We drink, we eat.

Scat

When will it end, and how
I wondered, as I listened to Ella sing
another verse to "Take the A Train."
She went her own way, running
the train, becoming the trumpet,
and though the song seemed forsaken
for her peerless syllables
she returned to catch the melody
the way filings swing
back to a magnet.

No wonder
my mother bought our first stereo
for my new father on his birthday.
He said he loved jazz
and he owned all the records
and maybe he really knew
the famous people he claimed
for friends.
A honey-colored door
opened to reveal
a turntable on springs
and no matter where you sat
you could hear music pour across
the room as if the band were playing
at his request.

I thought we might have to take it back
because the gift wasn't for him alone
and she must have spent his money
to buy a little happiness,
and because he beat her that night anyway;
but it stayed so we played it
until his shirts came home
from the Chinese laundry
stiff with forbidden starch,
tied in paper bundles
as if to hide the broken buttons

fused to scorched cuffs,
collars pointing to a tirade.

Tonight when I heard Ella sing
a song he must have listened to
a hundred times, I wondered if he was there
in the audience
I could hear applauding,
and I stayed in my car
until the song ended. I thought I might
forgive what he had done
now that the music he loved
made a claim on me. I told myself
scatting must have been his only
rebellion, uptown when he was blue
and downtown when he was lonely
but always back
to where he began,
his inescapable life.

He was afraid, clearly
afraid, when it came to the end.
He was younger than I am now,
and we passed each other
in the living room without
saying a word. I was late for school.
I could see he was troubled, weary
and lost. He was circling
unwelcome, worrisome terrain,
the familiar carpet underfoot forsook him;
with difficulty he lifted himself
up the steps and may have stumbled
before falling back to bed.
The birds formed distinct notes
on the wires outside the windows.
He cried out tunelessly.

Even in a Dream the Dead are like the Photograph Still Inside the Camera

Mother was pleased
by the small private collection
of Impressionists, including
the Christmas scene by Grandma
Moses. The blue sky!
That drew me. I was sad
the whole trip and not even
Chagall could enliven me
with his allure. His love for Bella
dispirited me. In this late painting
she has recently died
and his horse face is flayed.
The eyes are a conflagration.
He longed for her breasts
and had lavished his love
on their shape, youthful
and alike, the twin fawns
of Solomon's fruitful lust.

Mother's companion, a type
of late husband even at this
stage, shuffled agreeably
through one gallery into another.
To be with someone you've known
so briefly compared to your children
and grandsons, your departed, your
doctor—what is it but an aggravation
of daily proportion, epoch-less?

Yesterday at my nephew's party
upon becoming a man,
we waited to celebrate, as if by custom
on the coast of California,
in the historic nautical museum.
As the sun crashed into the surf
we had our drinks on the deck
in the cool summer air.

Then we were steered into the reception
amid the chaos of the children.
No one looked
at the cases of antique diving equipment.
The great gold helmet
weathered in an airless exhibit
sitting on a seabed of sand.
The ghostly absent diver
could feel the cold coming
through the canvas suit,
seeping inside the stiffened gloves.

When the sound track began
to the video of my nephew's life
it ushered in the hush. Teens drummed
the floor beneath crossed legs
as he appeared, newborn, like the advent
of a prophet held in his mother's
unsuspecting arms. My sister radiated serenity
and satisfaction, yet she looked
airbrushed into pornography,
soft focus, bathrobe, shot
rays of window light, as if
the rapture of birth had taken place
under a sprinkler.
We followed the family snorkeling
in the blue waters of Baja,
enjoying Hawaii, and recently France
with its bilious Seine below
their houseboat. I began to begrudge
the unending movie of life with children.
When my turn came
to appear in the film
each frame showed me surrounded
by nieces and nephews, wives
edited out; in the more recent years
the children cluster around me
on the beach or in the lobby, while I smile
like I'm wincing from the glare.

Would it help if I imagined
that my father, standing behind his camera
at the beach, the sea so small
in fits inside the view,
watched over me with imperishable
pleasure? I was a boy
when he became a handful of sand.

Death is that day on which
it makes no difference what
you choose to imagine.

Poem about a thumb

With my thumb I can gently brush away
       a drop of coffee on a cup
I can hold down the tuckpoint
       between the book's pages

or keep the tip straight
       at the tear's edge of a garlic clove
I can tighten the nipples' skin
       turn the volume up loud.

I can sweep the flake of ash
       from the marble mantle
where it has flown in the fire's draft
       like unmelted snow. I can take

the twig of hair away
       that fell on your forehead
without waking you. I can turn
       your chin sideways to kiss your cheek.

How marvelous to have grown up
       to be gentle, even for a moment.

2.

And when he saw a fig tree in the way, he came to it, and found nothing thereon, but leaves only, and said unto it, Let no fruit grow on thee henceforward for ever. And presently the fig tree withered away.

—Matthew 21:19

Outside the Bath

Those afternoons on Grand Street
when you prepared to go out,
you sat in the bath of the old house
whose basement I rented.

You were married and he was my teacher, too.
Mornings would find me
in your kitchen, where he stood
naked, white as bone, confident

as a ghost of his impression on me.
Now, after success, he was on the verge
of giving up. Nights, we would drink
and he would talk about the students

he believed would succeed, and in bed
after you and he had made love
and your cries drifted down to me
through the cold air return

he'd tell you their fortunes.
One night you spread all ten
of your poems on my floor. That year
his kind neglect touched us both.

I suppose that is why we would talk
while you bathed, why he never cared
or seemed to see me. The water
barely hid you, it dipped below

the curve of your chin, your hair
lifted above your neck. I remember
it was red, that you were red
at the tips of your flushed breasts

and between your legs a flame
wavered. You were most confident
naked. One day you turned to me

your unlucky face, said you'd decided

to have an affair. I agreed
to drive you there, to be the one
who knew. I was learning something, too.
The secret of poetry is cruelty, we quoted him.

Spite

The church was hot and dark that day.
Outside, through the rain, the sun shined for spite
lighting the haloes above the figures
that blazed in the stained glass.
My loosened suit hung from my thin frame
and my beautiful bride might as well not have come.

We had written the prayers, Isaiah saying, Come,
eat, drink milk for free, this is the day
the trees clap their hands. The program framed
with a woven vine the songs we selected, and despite
my Presbyterian vows, I'd break the glass
at our party, where I'd hold the slender figure

of my bride around the waist. I had figured
everything out, who'd sit where, and come
evening, counted my drinks by the glass
so at the end of the day
I'd not be too tired; but there was a spat
between mother and son that happened in freeze-frame.

Back in the church, the photographer wanted to frame
the moment before the guests arrived, where no figure
of effigy hung, at the pulpit, Jewish mother and son. Spite-
fully, or because I'd broken her heart, she would not come
forward, and after one step, faltered, stepping back. The day
went away. When I knelt at the altar like breaking glass

my loafers quivered, loosened on my heels. Last Supper's glass
of Passover wine spilled human blood, the frame-
up of sacrifice meant nothing—I was the betrayer that day—
and though the tenor's song in Hebrew would figure
in my failed plan, my friendly photographer saying, Come,
made my mother unhook her arm from mine. Now my spite

began to burn. The Christ candle wavered despite
the airless church, and with words of glass
I spoke my vows. All our friends had come

19

to see us wed. A deep chord moaned, shook the frame
of the organ, but I could not look at a figure
or a face—there was no one left in the church that day.

I still smiled like the figure in a frame
and broke the glass I intended to that day.
And full of spite, took her hand for a dance, *Come.*

Honeymoon

Just to say something beautiful
you put this word in your mouth
and then there is nothing
but what has befallen you
to talk about. *I remember*
is how it begins.
I remember the Bay of Fundy.
We went there to witness
the sea slip away
and the land remember the water
like a drained lake.
Shambling toward the beach stairs
of weathered decking
we pass cars from our country,
laughing when we see
the ubiquitous Jersey plate,
my home state, and then go down
flight by flight under dripping rocks
and roots shaking in the exposed
dirt, and soon the sign itself
that we are in some kingdom,
scarves of seaweed
draped over the railing
and dented sand
into which we sink.

Farther along the moonish beach
other rocks, pitted and indifferent,
look like they know
twenty-five feet of the sea
feels like nothing at all.
We want them to love us, I think,
or we want to love them
before our visit ends
but the cold white sky
looks uninviting and suddenly
we feel too small
to endure the new world.

Hand in hand we walk through
Hopewell Rock still dripping
seawater, knowing that soon
the bay will pour in here
then pour out again
and that for us there is no saving
what was already missing
when we came.

In the familiar photograph
that fills a few inches of the Sunday
Times magazine section,
a man with his pants rolled
like a clam digger,
a woman in a pink sweater,
her hair drifting from its knot
at the back of her neck,
with the water again withdrawn,
I see the horizon that you and I
walked before and I feel the belief
we shared at the disjuncture
of land and sky, as if at the end
of every argument
there would be this remembrance
as of the Christ candle
lit at our wedding.
As if it were burning still.

We drove on toward Nova Scotia,
toward Kejimikujic, the lit waters
of summer, the long, drafty
laugh of the loons. I remember
a day we couldn't decide
whether to stop or drive
and we argued till the cold
ocean appeared and I pulled over.
We walked toward an inlet
greasy with boat spillage
and the sun in oily eclipse
so that I could swim

while you stayed by the shore
almost pacing
as I stroked and lifted
what trailed like crystal
in the wet light. Eastward
a shallow moon trilled
and rose in the grey sky.
I still feel the need
to say something beautiful
though we are through with belief
and this picture of a beach
serves only to sell
a place where the signs of love
seem plentiful. I think
of all that has been withdrawn
as if we had blown out
our own candle and that little
feather of smoke stings the eyes.
Still, it is spring again
and the newly turned earth
brings back what had only
retreated. Someone starts
a lawnmower and doesn't curse
but blesses the ceaseless grass.
The birds are windows that open
after long seasons, rope creaking
up a windless well.

Barren

I found a tick there
in the loose skin that hangs,
days after returning from the woods
of a state park in Missouri.
It was full summer, signs warned hikers
to stay away from the brush, wear
pants tucked into socks, and explore
the body you bathe when you return;
for even a speck of dirt
that you can't flick away
or even a freckle
can turn inward and grow.

Like the poppy-thin skin of a man's cheek
whose old body has puckered,
like the milky pod
that dangles from a sapless limb,
like the fig tree Jesus withered,
like seedfruit and breadfruit
but not a flower and not a fruit
the testicle deceives.
What purpose, what wisdom
and what end contained
in the sightless process
led us here, where our limits
come up like an empty net,
a purse seine drawn together
by our two boats
to be a sign of prosperity, to feed us
for our labors,
to close upon sea water.

I thought a miracle might happen.

Sarah must wait forever, it seems,
and learning she will bear a son
laughs and barely escapes
more wrath. Rebecca's womb

is closed for a time
though in a world where time
stretched on and on
it seemed forever
she was denied children
as numerous as the sand
or the stars that cover heaven
or the dust that spreads across
the dry and barren land.
Like Jacob I labored
to make someone mine.
For a time we believed
God would grant us children
if only I forgave. But
unlike Jacob I was mistaken.
The stone upon the well
was very heavy, and
she who married me waited
while I moved it aside, but
the well was dry. Dear
tick, hanging black as a seed,
suck deep, drink, grow fat
from me, be a life
that I have fed, that found
its way to my body,
then fall, be fruitful, and multiply.

Failed Attempt

One web that wasn't there before
hangs above the gate when I come home.
It crackles like brittle glass
as I tear it out of my hair,
unstitch it from my mouth like spun sugar.
Yesterday that spider wove
while a thunderstorm assembled
over the Mississippi and split the sky
into a cathedral ceiling. The visible planes
of air in the web opened into space
at the octagon where the spider walked.

Tonight I know that something from the past
has touched me, is above me and knows
that I am afraid. If I look up
I can see the circling river of the sky.
I am moved by a chilly, rank kiss
across the courtyard and wet grass
to touch the fence just finished.
Yellow in daylight, it is now
only a scent, cedar and pepper,
drawing me blindly against its rough face
where my fear stops as though a father
rubbed his unshaven cheek across my cheek
to make a point about being a man.

And I know that somewhere the last night
of a love now ending
is weaving itself together, intricate fate
like a web even now I feel flutter.
That which I wait upon, I devour.
That which waits upon me, devours me.

Desolated

It's possible to live on the surface
of life, as on a pond,
the way Travis in *Taxi Driver* does.
Alone in his room
he takes notes, keeps a journal
on all that he abjures.
It is as if the war we haven't seen him fight
outfits him to stay awake
and keep distance, always, between himself
and the next likely victim. One snowy night
the weather made us close, as in a carriage,
and next day, bundled into sausages,
we crunched through high, new snow
into the destined park.
A few giddy drivers
rewarded themselves
for buying jeeps and trucks.
The woods were quiet, but the wind burned.
We were indivisible in our task
to climb a small hill.
Alike on the landscape though apart
we let the breath out of the snow
with each heave
as we fell step by step
through the crust that had formed
in the hour of the ice.
The muscles of your thighs were tired,
your ankles warm with pain;
there were your dark enormous eyes,
the same untiring face
that never expressed resolve or dismay
as though you'd absorbed blows
and shuddered surprise
into stillness like a fighter
learning where the pain came from
and how to avoid it.
When we crouched down
at a windbreak, between

27

the frozen stems of tow-headed reeds
bent over by the ice,
I wished, simply, that we had
kissed. But I did not kiss you
and you did not kiss me.
What good, then, was that storm
for all its change?

The Bond

Tonight the half-cup
of a girl's bathing suit
the moon beckons to me
from above the trees,
pulling away to shine alone.
When I come inside
my wife is studying
two models of molecules
placed on the table.
Carbon, I think,
but then I see that each tilts
missing an electron,
heavy with particles
though unstable.
The trick, she says,
is to picture the bond
as a struggle,
strength being relative
to pulling away.

This morning I watched
two cardinals
chase each other,
red on red
going for the same
female, then
in a thicket
bare with winter,
her dull attraction
to his
earned achievement. Victory
made him sing.
She flew away
and he to her,
she appeared
distracted and he intent,
they balanced
on twigs, the tails

fluttered, the snow,
fused to the ground
below the bush,
by midday slipped
away like shed skin.
By virtue
of their feathers
they have mastered flight
but stay still
a moment. Come spring
the fragile eggs
strike like matches,
fall open, cupped
and white.

3.

Belly

"...and she said to Jacob, 'Give me children, or I shall die!'"

—Genesis 30:1

1.

I wish it were medicine in the nightly injection
but you are not ill. The needles
in their safe box lie
side by side, a little ill-fitting
as logs on a millpond.

And some dark weather lumbers in
with each shot, same hour of evening
to cloud the countenance, though I play
doctor, asking after the patient,
promising a bright future.

Chances are good if we divide
by two, then divide again,
we'll be indivisible. Aqua vitae,
water of life, enhancing elixir, self-
improvement. We're making up nature's future.

2.

Your body is heavy as will happen
with hope, its languor. I work out
to dispel it. Sitting this evening in the steam
room, among big naked men with relaxed
penises and shoulders, I felt drawn down

inward toward my navel, and even breathing
a deep breath didn't fill me up.
I sat, stiff-backed, in my cloud
and saw through steam all men
winging on wide shoulders like maple seeds.

3.

All at once, I'm all for it
eager as a tomcat to be let out
at night. *Let's do it.*

You set up another syringe
which I flick and tap
to dislodge air. Your part, to be

beyond the pain I bring.
You make me promise
to glide this ice

against your belly
where it burns
until you feel numb.

I pinch you
with one hand, with the other
uncap the needle

to reveal the 45° bevel
cut as in a marrow bone
sharpened to a point,

turn it so the spear
will pierce your skin.
Then I draw back for blood.

None filters in
to fog the clear liquid.
The plunger slides in an instant.

Good body, take
and distribute this element.
Make ready. Life hides.

4.   *Milk*

Longing is the loss
commensurate with lack;
nothing really is gone,
yet nothing has come

of the effort and need
except a steady aspect,
like a face always at a bar
over a drink never ending. *Freshen*

I asked the poets last night,
is it a word, to freshen?
The rain freshens, the cows
freshen when they begin to milk.

5.   *Shard*

What are they doing to you?
Capture. Harvest.
Lately you feel sexless.

They are ripening you.
Retrieval. Cryogeny.
The environment surrenders

to an instigation.

6.   *Belly*

These are yours, like the little hairs
seen underwater, how they lift
and feather along the length of an arm
or from the thigh seem to swim

in the passing current, everything slow
and still until a disturbance
reaches the shallow where a limb
or wrecked spar settles, almost seethes,

in dust. Which is sand, which is
blue brine, a cloud passing its shadow
over a field, as a float drifts across
a bed of kelp, as my hand eclipses

the gold, now sallow, belt of shore
of your belly under the bright light.
How you see me see you, sparse school
of hairs like imperceptible fish

crossing my sight, your flesh illuminated
too brightly, small coins of bruise.
Pinch harder, you say. Between thumb and forefinger
I guide the needle's sharpened keel, and your eyes swim.

7.   *Classroom*

Somewhere on this arc, in this ultimate curve,
there must be a place for destiny.

I sidle beside you, scoot the stool close,
and lean to kiss your revered belly.

Little regions of blame have appeared,
small countries of expectation

into which we marshal this leading edge
of hope. It's harrowing even to expect outcome.

Guest of your planned feast,
your belly bedecked like a picnic,

I drink a few glasses of wine to will myself
to come to you for fortune or favor.

Others do differently. Our friends, for instance,
can go home and fuck frightened of consequence.

I had forgotten, now that your body seems to be
the fallow field, the reason you go through this;

you are fertile as the Egypt of your birth.
The first blood appears, suggesting the drugs work.

We are destiny.

Dismissed.

8.

Secrets unfold
       in the most casual way, harmless
as watching daylight fade

and turn to dust among the trees.
       Sunday ends. Back in bed
the lovers, careless of caution, rest their heads

on the deep, settled pillows. Twice
       the phone rang, and then they returned
their faces to their kiss,

as when one enters
       the water on a daylong stay,
the light now different, the cove a little colder.

In the afterward
       as trees quilt and unfocus
and we gaze through the windows we left undrawn

into middle distance seeing not much
       beyond our stilled longing,
diminished,

we discuss a little blithely
       relaxed and cool to the touch
the day our desire may end.

The taste of the lake
       on our skin, or so the scent seemed
when it rose, brought up other lovers

who in their likeness to our plight
          decidedly seemed victorious
leaving our fate uncertain. If,

you said, we reach a point
          where the passion doesn't return,
we must let each other know

so as not to live in despair.
          It was time to dress, to drink,
and we rolled away to separate sides.

Both of us uncovered, quelled,
          I didn't steal a glance
as I often did. We were reaching the stage

when, if the woman's ovaries retained
          the fullness the drugs intended,
foreshadowing the capture of an egg,

she would not be allowed
          even the shudder of her coming.
Chances were all we had, and the first

might be the best. I wasn't afraid
          of restraint. I should have been
but something in your honesty, or your demeanor

when you'd counted the number
          of lovers you had taken
or foreswore a future without desire,

made me calm.

9.   *Fragment*

She can't believe
it's over. Come in
to find her crying. Put down
that plate of quartered hearts—

it might as well be the thistle
of the artichoke served her.
Resort to falling
beside her on the bed

Three Storms

Morning

It is so cold, we can not hear the birds.

I no longer know what constitutes hope.

The first sip of water in near daylight.

The clink of the heat coming back again

or night, as it leaves, like a flourished cape.

To love, one must control one's emotions.

Yes—it is not the other way around.

The coffee fogs like film beside the guitar

hollow and alone, leaned in the corner.

The old love there like a wound to return to.

As a light unplugged or a bulb not lit

yet—nothing is but what was and will be.

(three storms)

From a Window

What do these rooftops seen through winter trees

mean today, the brown-gold grasses, the wind

whistling through the window as dusk falls?

It's cold in here as coffee in the cup.

There is that worthless crow again, sexless.

Somewhere in the distance a great cornfield

shatters and stubble rows burst with birds.

Evening settles on Illinois. Prairies

like women stepping out of the bath freeze.

Beneath a blanket a woman might be

a man. The heaving curves curled to sleep

lie still. We have all grown dark with the world.

(three storms)

Love

Season for this, season for that, it snows.

What has afternoon been doing to you

since you've been away? Can I count on you?

After this christening why want the snow gone

when it has come like a gift unbidden

crazy in its plenitude? Look out

your window. Fire escape reaching the brick

building's roof, the vent stack warping smoke

weightless on its ladder, articulate

almost as a prayer—if you . . . would you . . .

home alone, peace-filled, almost, not quite, cured.

4.

*For what we cannot accomplish, what
is denied to love,
    what we have lost in the anticipation—
        a descent follows,
endless and indestructible* .

—William Carlos Williams

At the Artists' Colony

Drought. The grasses whipping
the blood red briars
latent and sapless, chidden,
unbudded. Before
I came into the field
away from the others
I walked with a painter
down the dry road
kicking up pebbles.
The wild turkeys flushed so suddenly
I was glad
to have started them
and to watch, nothing more,
as they took to the trees
to pay no attention to me.
Here, I give you
the thin blue river
visible at her temple.

Written On a Subscription Blank

Night after night I push the small button
on the radio, an hour for music
to guide me to sleep.
If I dream, my head in the valley
between two long pillows, if I waken to
neighbors fighting again, the sound of one hurting
the other, if I thirst, if I snore
or fart, or appear to have fallen onto the bed
from a great height, if I waken and can't move
a limb, if I call out, or if I pass
from unconsciousness into a kingdom
where women call to me with their hands upturned
imploring, kneading the air like dough—
how many years of such quiet emptiness
lacking futurity
will it take my life to arrive?

Affair

Treasure in the mission
to Mars movies. The one man
in the crew who steals away to find
a cave in the mountain where there's no
god, where the sun when it arrives
casts a line in the sand you know
he's going to cross. Does it matter
as long as he stays in the shade
he can fill his pockets with jewels?
In no time
once he steps into the light
his bones appear where his spacesuit had been
leaving the sumptuous rubies, red but strangely cool,
like the poured out heart, wasted there,
of no avail.

Vichy

I call that plant Vichy, because it is a great plant
but it is in part a collaborator. Look how it spears
the air, long variegated fronds of agave
reaching toward the sky. It keeps to itself
all that has ever rumbled in its roots. I like it
and once in a while turn it
sunward, drenching its darker side, revealing it
to be small, dwarfed where no one is looking.
Who left this plant to me is now long since gone.
When she does call I get drawn in,
am asked the sorts of questions to which
only the wrong answer is right. Such as
do you miss me, and the follow up to it,
I mean really miss me. Then someone says *yes*
who I feel is not me. Later I can tell the truth
but for now it is best to comply. And to know
that even though I am captive I must protect
my captor. I subtly turn the conversation
back toward the one she has gone to, gone over
as if to the other side, and she seems to brighten,
as today, in the chill house and the emptiness
I turn Vichy toward the light.

My Wife's Black Bra

The rain had dragged the magnolia blossoms down
like sad mouths. The sun came out again.
I decided to do the laundry.

I went to the basement, opened the dryer
and took a few things out, full of sparks.
In the arms of a fleece I found my wife's

black bra attached by electricity, the empty satin
cups I could imagine holding her. Once more
I was filled with wonder and struggle.

I didn't know what to make of wanting
an opportunity again with the body
I had forsaken. I began to sense

her presence, the way she moved her hair aside
only to let it fall, how her lips
looked ripe, as if she'd just been kissed.

I thought of her striding the long hallway
to my office after hours, dusk
during the hard dark of February, and then, right there

the pencils in their cup trembling, the phone sensing a tremor.
I put the bra aside to face the plunge
of hot water, this much detergent, the dirty whites.

5.

Regular as sun and moon, in the middle of burning summer, without a drop of rain in sight, when all other rivers on earth were drying up, for no apparent reason at all, the Nile rose out of its bed every year, and for three months embraced all of Egypt.

— "The Last Nile Flood," John Feeney

Steppe

You remember loving people
—uncles who were fathers' friends,
an aunt who came each day with bread
and cookies, walking her crooked step
past the bakery. You were her brother's
child and your mother his widow.
That step of hers in black
shoes.
          A bird woman,
her knobbed hands and black eyes,
her hair still black, how brightly
she loved you, in place of your father,
so you wouldn't know he was gone.
You can love someone this way
when you don't expect anything
in return.
              Don't call it
a virtue though. Grief powers it
the way a generating station lights
a town in the remote cold.

The Snow

Now they're collecting the snow
we awaited so expectantly
and for which we have only one word.
Here we do not say snow before nightfall,
wet snow of rush hour, snow
like new dimes or snakes on a dry highway,
snow like cake
rising on the branch,
unforgivable spring snow
burning magnolia blossoms, shivering
in the throat of a crocus, snow that hurts
the eyes, that makes you want to turn
away, snow that falls on the tongue
of the ocean,
snow that squeaks, snow that whispers,
that no longer stirs the limbs
of lovers, snow of parting
falling on two, one lonely
and one in love with snow,
crazy snow circling around
like a father who can't find his child,
that makes the night too bright
to sleep; inconsolable
snow that falls upon
a widow's veil and melts
as she walks from the garden
of stone, snow
that makes the night a negative,
snow on her already
purchased plot, snow in the grove
of flameless cedars.

One kind of snow to be dispensed with
the day after.

Sympathy

for C.D.

All the long morning that became today
I worried that I'd seen a sign
when I walked myself sober in the Sunday chill.
A patch of bedraggled tulips—it seemed
like a pond—was drenched with an abundance
of rain, while all around it seemed dry.

But it wasn't the abundance of moisture
pouring from the tipped cups of the tulips.
It was their fallen petals like portals
let down to allow a queen to leave.
Or the flowers had drowned.
They were hidden in a grotto-like glade

where the brewery workers were meant to spend
a quiet lunch forgetting their labors
in the sleepy spring air. There were red
and white striped tulips, and there were black
ones that might have been purple
before the hour of the rose.

The heads of the flowers flowed together
like hair weeping down a girl's face,
same sadness, same sorrow and degradation
as if her body had been abused.
The soil was raised in a mound and still rich
but the season was over. Sympathy

is a good name for the look of the tulips
all leaning over upon one another.
Immediately I felt the impact, I would say,
of their faces, how they would not really
look up again, even into the bright morning.
I felt that way when you came off the plane

and I saw your face again after twelve years.
You moved toward me in the terminal

and came forward through the crowd. Now your hair
was all silver. When I saw your pale blue eyes
I knew you again. For the few days we were together
I studied the changes in your face.

I held you in my arms one night, to dance
the blues, the last song of the last set
we'd hear before we left, maybe the last time
we'd ever touch. Now we moved to a tempo
no one could keep, but we held tight
and I worried a little that we danced poorly together.

Were we being watched? I tried to turn us
toward the face and fingers of Johnny Johnson
so you could admire him. Our bodies revolved
in an orbit on the dance floor. It seemed
perfect to be in love with you again, to have spent
the whole day wandering through the city.

Today I wondered if we had said enough
that there was no future. I took the usual
Sunday morning walk, asserting my way.
I hurt worst at the moment I observed
the tulips from the distance. I went forward
into their pull. I could sense them speaking

the way their subtle sodden motions
mimicked a crowd of mourners, their heads bent
toward the end. You can see
why I would say this was a sign, then that it wasn't.
I thought this flock of tulips could speak, then knew it couldn't.
I walked away, then late in the day called you one last time.

Nothing goes here

My body part goes
inside your body part
a key goes inside a lock
a hand, etc., its glove
the gasoline goes inside the tank
and the nozzle goes back to the square-
shouldered pump the dollars
go into the register
the milk goes in the glass
the knife in the chest some
know what that feels like
the dying know what it means
to pass beyond the need
for a mirror   to know themselves
as they at last are
the body goes inside the coffin
a weevil goes inside the bole
a worm enters the cabbage
rides the waxen waves
the sound goes into the whorls
of the ear
the seed goes inside the pit
inside the womb
a father goes in the wake of the seed
a mother goes in the take of the egg

but in my house
alone at the end of the week
the last hour of the week
Sunday midnight
small red lamp on the mantle
the static of silence
nothing goes here

Silk

Yellow and heavy, one last ray poured
Into a fresh bouquet of dahlias
And hardened there.

Anna Akhmatova

I chose the flowers quickly
the day I came to see you
home from hospital,
your baby on your breast,
and I waited downstairs until
I was asked for. I didn't wish
to see you like that, wearied,
torn, your clothes disarrayed
as though a storm swept through
and you—and *this*—remained.
Arriving in the room, I saw
from a distant door I once
had called my own, you there
in the corner far away and small.
I thought to see, when my eyes sharpened
in the window light
to shut out all I couldn't
take, the father, lounging in silk.
He slept on in the next room
and you were as you were. For you
waiting in my arms as if I carried
the cut-down, tendered blooms
across a rain swell or a wave
washed ashore from wherever
the unwanted go or come back from,
the vivid, foolish, clown-faced daisies,
the coarse, lumescent, faintly ghoulish
metallic petals of the eucalyptus.

The Last Nile Flood

I stopped to watch the horses today
as they lingered in their pastures
of mud and straw, the fence worn
and thorny. In the distance behind them
a bulldozer listed, rusting
in the quiet air. One horse was white
with ribs showing, a back swayed
as a clothesline heavy with wet shirts;
the horse's sides were dirty white
and a bit threadbare, like a worn out rug.
He seemed content, busy biting the grass
poorly sprouting in a field of dirt;
he kept his mouth close to the ground
clipping the snips of grass with lazy ease.
In the next pasture, like a sight you shouldn't see,
a brown mare lay on the ground. I thought
she was dead and gone, and for a long time
I watched to see her side rise
like a ship on a swell, the huge ribs
unmoving, the hooves crossed as a woman
might cross her ankles leisurely to suggest
interest and calm, and just like that
she awoke and startled me, the elegant
unconcern with which she raised her head,
enormous as a swan's unfolded wings,
sleek as a seal in the sunshine, turning
like a searchlight her wide brown eye;
she rose so high but no more. I waited
to see the trouble she would go to, to know
what pull I exerted, a tall two-footed post
behind a makeshift fence of hard wire.
I wanted to see first one fore hoof planted
and the great neck extended, the long nose
with a streak of paint drawn down between the eyes
to the black mask of her nostrils;
and the struggle to get up, awkward but
then accomplished, the body as whole
and brown as a grand piano. But no.

The white swayback went on munching
in the first warm rays of the day, early spring
still chill and bleak. The greening alders
seemed like smoke throughout the woods;
everywhere a yellow bush burned through
and on the slope the spun white field grasses
lay down like the waters of Nile,
which years ago flooded for the last time.

Cheat

Now the flowers taper out
like matches held in the hand
and another summer day gives off
its breath of exhaustion and ash.

Under the trees we turn the pram
toward the church of white stone.
All the skateboarders are gone,
back in school and bored.

We talk and I see the dim, cracked stars
but the only thing
I hear is the crickets sing
their one word, *cheat*.

I remember lying
under the motorcycle, then sitting up
cursing into the closed shell
of my deafened helmet, a car

backing slowly away, afraid.
The impact and result, then
the shaking of the aftershock.
The seal I broke.

Back in your apartment you ask
would I like to see the baby's
first bath, just after delivery
when the father's shaky hand

caught the way it felt to have
to wait; the nurse's patient
disregard of the baby's unendurable
cry, and your voice, your face

exhausted but beautiful
like summer's last exhalation
of self-regard before

we admit it's over. Look at me

now, tender and thrifty
with myself, I almost feel
like falling in love again;
as when one has been gravely

injured and for the first minutes
before awakening to a dark stain
spreading across the chest
attempts to help someone.

After the Rain

Everything is wet
this morning after the rain.
The needles of the white pine
are fattened with drops
like beads along a string.
Now a wind passes over
waking the old oaks
and it sounds like rain
returning. I remember
summer days
when young, how bored
I was yet happy
that we could not work
on the wet wood
of a half-framed house.
At home, between semesters,
full of feeling
like a dare,
I'd wait for the rain
to let up
and it would return
wave upon wave
as if it were tireless
or unsatisfied.
I've known desire
once, maybe more
than once, to feel
like that, and I've held on
for its return, waiting
with the rain's
thirst.
The red leaves of the maple
under the lens of the sun
through the bright water
are not red at all,
more like a child's finger
held to a flashlight
almost flayed, as when

you come upon hunger
and its work in the woods.
The air is that of a sea
coast, just above the waves,
whitened with a bright mist
so that the birds, too,
are whitened, bleached
of detail, an Aegean
whiteness, except for the trees
drenched and heavy.

When the rain lifted
there was the next day's
work to worry about
and the refusal to love
anything. The wet lumber
squeaked with nails
and squirted when the hammer
hit and there was silence
most of the day. I remember
the smell of sugar
and amber, of pulp
and the darkened sap
of knots, the weight
of plywood against my shoulder
and palm as I climbed
the ladder to the bare roof
and laid it down
relieved of fear, then
did it again. So much
for the white dress
of a summer bride
and her hair woven
with rain. Afternoons
asleep on the sofa
for an hour after work,
I'd wake and cry out
for my life, certain
I'd missed the day.

6.

Outside the window is the next of everything.

—W. S. Merwin

Forecast

Funny I should think of telling you about
the rain.   You're in England, a rainy island.

I would like to talk about a few things.

I would like to hold your child.

It occurs to me that if I were to write "I
would like to hold our child," how tragic
my whole life would seem.

A rainy island!

You should hear it now, it isn't rain
anymore, it's hitting hard on the windows
and sweeping the streets, trees swaying
and swamping like a capsized boat, because
hail is flying.

Oh, but it's over so fast, things quietening,
the river overtaking some bridge.

I think too of the woman I slept with this year,
how she hates thunder and whether I should
call her.   But you know what,

that voice that makes me call her
is not around tonight.

A quiet, declining rainy night.

You're over in England. You sent me some
pictures.

You said, "Hi, Family."

ABOUT THE AUTHOR

STEVEN SCHREINER is the author of the collection *Too Soon to Leave* and the chapbook *Imposing Presence*, and co-author with Allison Cundiff of *In Short, a Memory of the Other on a Good Day*. His poems have appeared in many magazines, including *Poetry*, *Image*, *Colorado Review*, *River Styx* and *December*, and numerous anthologies. He is the recipient of fellowships from the VCCA, Tall Rock Retreat, and The National Writer's Voice of the YMCA. He teaches in the MFA Program at the University of Missouri-St. Louis and is the founding editor of *Natural Bridge, a journal of contemporary literature*.

CPSIA information can be obtained at www.ICGtesting.com
Printed in the USA
BVOW08s0329150316

440351BV00002B/16/P